gethsemani

A LIFE OF PRAISE

EX LIBRIS · EX LIBRIS · EX LIBRIS · EX LIBRIS

JOSEPH F. KOZAR, S.M.

Text by Thomas Merton

*A*ll Christians are called to a life of perfect charity and service in imitation of Jesus Christ. Some Catholics, in order to devote themselves more wholeheartedly to the quest of perfection and union with God, take religious vows and follow the way of the evangelical counsels.

Among the various forms of dedicated life which are well known in the Catholic Church, monasticism has a special character of its own. A contemplative monastery has no other purpose than the praise and love of God. It does not exist in order to carry out any other task, however useful. Even if nobody knew they were there, the monks would continue to live for God, seeking to honor Him to please Him alone.

This direct service to God for His own sake is in fact the earliest form of consecrated life in the Church, apart of course from the life of priest and bishop. As early as the fourth century A.D. Christians withdrew into the deserts of Egypt and Syria in order to live alone with God. This did not however mean that they severed all contact with the rest of the human race: though solitary they maintained relations among themselves, even though they did not always form communities, and they offered hospitality to the rare travellers who came their way. However, living alone in the desert, in silence, and without the comforts and advantages of ordinary social life, they discovered new dimensions in the way of sacrifice and prayer. They gained deep insight into the human mind and man's interior conflicts, as well as a new understanding of divine grace and the mystery of God's love for man in Christ. Their wisdom and humility taught them the way to interior peace. After such qualified observers as St. Athanasius and other Fathers of the Church had seen the value of the monastic way, it became recognized in the Church as a most perfect vocation. The monk left all in order to respond perfectly to the words of Jesus: "If anyone wishes to come after me let him deny himself and take up his cross and come follow me: for whoever wants to save his life will lose it, and whoever loses his life for my sake will find it." (Matthew 16:24-25).

Of course there are many different ways of putting this teaching of Christ into effect, but the early monks thought that to leave the advantages and pleasures of social life, to be entirely forgotten and unknown to the rest of the world, in order to live in silence, sacrifice and

prayer, was the best way of facing the deepest realities of life and of giving oneself entirely to God.

As time went on, the austere simplicity of the early desert life became modified and monasticism developed into an institution taking various forms. One kind of monasticism placed emphasis on pure solitude with a minimum of organization. Monks who lived entirely alone were known as hermits and gave themselves entirely to contemplation. Since a completely solitary life has dangers and disadvantages, most monks preferred to live in communities and were known as cenobites, or monks living a 'common life', emphasizing asceticism, liturgy and work.

The monastic community forms a family of disciples gathered around an Abbot or 'spiritual Father' who is not merely a juridical head and superior but also represents Christ and teaches the other monks the way of holiness. Obedience to the Abbot and fraternal love for his fellow disciples enable the cenobite to follow more closely the way of humility and love which is that of Christ and of the Gospel. The monastic community is committed to self support by manual labor, to a simple life of poverty and silence, and to separation from the world. Isolation, enclosure and silence give the monk a certain solitude even though he is living in community.

Monastic community life took many different historical forms. In the Middle Ages, some monasteries became great social and religious institutions and played a very influential role in political and cultural history. They became training centers for bishops and religious leaders, as well as refuges for scholarship and the intellectual life in an age of crisis and conflict. Other monasteries later rejected this influential role because it involved too much social activity and interfered with the peace and silence of the monastic vocation.

However, some communities, founded in non-Christian areas felt bound to preach the Gospel and turned to necessary pastoral work. After evangelizing whole areas of Europe, they remained in contact with the people, preaching and teaching them, though this was not part of the primitive monastic ideal. It is nevertheless one traditional development of monasticism.

Hence we can say there are roughly four kinds of monastic life in

existence in the Western Church today. There are a few communities of semi-hermits. There are cenobitic communities which emphasize silence, manual labor, penance and contemplation. There are still others which devote themselves more to liturgical prayer and to the intellectual life, while of course retaining monastic silence and solitude. Finally there are others which devote themselves almost entirely to pastoral and educational work, while also emphasizing liturgical worship, particularly in its pastoral aspect.

The present book enables you to see something of the life of one of the oldest monastic communities in the Western hemisphere, the Abbey of Gethsemani. This is a community of Cistercian Monks of the Strict Observance, popularly known as 'Trappists' (a name taken from the monastery of La Grande Trappe in Normandy).

The Cistercians have traditionally been an austere Order of monks, famed for their silence, their withdrawal from the world, their manual labor and their penance. The Cistercian life is essentially and before all else a life of prayer and penance. But prayer and penance can take different outward forms. Without changing the essence of their life, the Cistercian monks are, like all other religious Orders, engaged in re-thinking and re-planning some of the accidental approaches to their basic aim. This adjustment is a result of the Second Vatican Council.

THE SPIRIT OF GETHSEMANI

Dom James Fox

Founded before the Civil War, in 1848, the Abbey of Gethsemani has seen many changes in its relatively long history. The founders of the monastery came from the Abbey of Melleray, in France. Melleray, on the borders of Brittany and near the region of Vendee, was recruited largely from these intensely Catholic areas which, during the French Revolution and after, remained fiercely attached to their faith. Gethsemani itself was founded as a refuge, at a time when the Motherhouse feared possible suppression in another revolutionary era, that of the mid-nineteenth century. From the very beginning, then, Gethsemani has been marked by a certain sense of crisis.

The rugged, austere quadrangle of old buildings, erected during the Civil War (in which a battle was fought at Perryville, not far away), took on an air of grim defiance. The founding French monks, who had crossed the Atlantic in a sailing ship to New Orleans and ascended the Mississippi and Ohio by river boat, insisted on keeping their strict rule in all its austerity even though the Kentucky climate made this very difficult. However, higher superiors imposed certain adjustments. Nevertheless the early monks continued to treat themselves without mercy, in a spirit of violent self-contempt characteristic of La Trappe. In historical perspective, this appears to have been unrealistic. One of the main consequences was that the Abbey attracted few vocations, and for fifty years its continued existence was in doubt. Finally, with the end of the century, the community was in such straits that it was ready to close down.

However, Dom Edmond Obrecht, an Alsatian Trappist trained at La Grande Trappe, saved the Gethsemani community from extinction and over a period of nearly forty years built it up into a prosperous and well-known Abbey. The rule of Dom Edmond was severe, as was that of his predecessors. But with a more flexible outlook he transformed Gethsemani into an American community, which proved that the ascetic life was not alien to U.S. Catholicism. The men of that day remain as

examples of American monks who were trained in a hard school of obedience and humiliation.

Dom Frederic Dunne, successor to Dom Obrecht and first American Abbot of Gethsemani, was a man of profound piety and kindness, but he interpreted the Rule and Trappist customs with an even more literal strictness than his predecessor. Yet under his abbotship the community suddenly began to grow. The phenomenal increase in American Cistercian vocations after World War II is one of the curious facts of U. S. Church history. The increase continued under the present Abbot, Dom James Fox and eventually reached a high point of two hundred and seventy-five in 1952.

This great influx of postulants which took the Order by surprise, was not an unmixed blessing. The first reaction of the community was to make several new foundations, in Georgia, Utah, South Carolina, and then in New York and California. These monasteries are now flourishing on their own. Gethsemani meanwhile coped with the problem of numerous postulants by intensified screening and a more prolonged and complete monastic formation.

At the same time, the rush of postulants diminished and the situation is now stabilized. There is no question that the hundreds of young Americans who have presented themselves at the gate of Gethsemani seeking admission, have been moved by an authentic desire for a life alone with God. In many cases they have reacted against the confusion and moral anarchy of life in an affluent society.

However, the monastic life is no escape from conflict. On the contrary, conflict must be faced more squarely in the monastery than anywhere else. It is a paradox that the man who cannot live with himself in the world will be still less able to live with himself in the monastery. Besides, the intense communal life of the monastery calls for great adaptability, tolerance, commonsense and fraternal charity.

The life of the Gethsemani community has been greatly modified in the last fifteen years. The General Chapter of the Order began making significant changes in the early nineteen fifties, in order to adjust the customs of our monasteries to the needs and mentality of modern man.

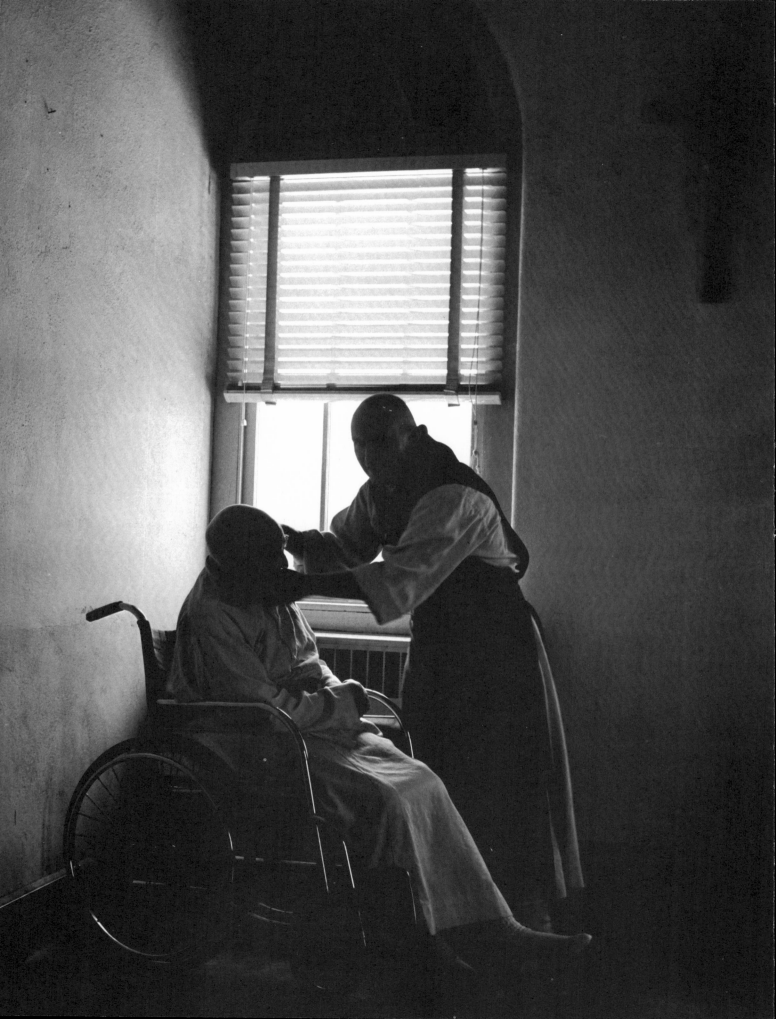

Community prayers added to the divine office were dropped. Some antique and purely medieval customs were quietly abandoned. The garments of the monks were simplified. The diet, while remaining vegetarian, was amplified. The strict confinement which kept everyone within the limits of the buildings was relaxed so that monks could go for walks by themselves in the woods on Sundays and Feast Days. The farm was reorganized and put on a completely modern basis. The study and intellectual life of the community was also given a more vital and meaningful character. Above all, the liturgy and chant were developed and perfected. With the liturgical reforms of Vatican II, these changes were of course intensified.

The introduction of a daily concelebrated Mass largely in English, has called for the creation of entirely new musical texts (based on Gregorian). With the prospect of an English choral office, the life of praise is taking on an entirely new aspect at Gethsemani. The monastic basilica is to be renovated to provide an appropriate setting for the new worship.

If the founders of Gethsemani were to see it today, they would scarcely believe their eyes.

*T*he monastic life is not one of idleness and inertia, nor is it devoted merely to reflection and introspection. There is always plenty for a monastic community to do, and sometimes the monks feel that there is not really enough time in which to do it. A monk must live by the labor of his hands, said St. Benedict, (*Rule,* c. 48) in order to imitate the first monastic Fathers and the Apostles. Hard work in the fields, gardens and shops of the monastery, or in the necessary maintenance of the monastery itself, keeps the monk's prayer life in touch with everyday reality. At the same time, the monk is also obliged to work with his mind, to study, to think, to deepen his understanding of the mysteries of faith and of monastic life itself. Thus two kinds of exacting and productive effort are demanded of the monk, manual labor and intellectual work. These two take up the time that the monk does not spend either in choral or secret prayer.

The monk may spend four to six hours a day in manual work, sometimes more. The horarium is now arranged to admit of a flexible work schedule with more time allotted to manual labor in case of those who need it. All must however share in a minimum amount of productive work, four hours a day, thus contributing to the support of the community.

The monastic farm is now highly mechanized and the planting, cultivation and harvesting of crops no longer occupy the whole work force of the monastery as they used to in former days. There are nevertheless many jobs on the farm, in the dairy and cattle barns, in the bakery as well as in carpentry, electrical, plumbing, shoemaking, and other shops, in the garage, the bookstore, and above all the 'farms building' where Gethsemani Farms products are processed and packaged. Building and renovation keep the construction crew busy year by year. In addition there are secretarial and accounting jobs to be done, not to mention teaching, and the considerable work that goes into the preparation of new musical texts for use in choir. Of course there is the Guest House to be taken care of, confessors and retreat masters are needed for retreatants, as well as cooks and other helpers. There is a monastic infirmary where the old and sick monks are provided for. Even this does not exhaust the list of jobs. The monastery has its own dental clinic, its own resident doctor and psychiatrist, a photographic studio, a printing shop, an artist, and a couple of authors.

All the monks are obliged by their vocation to continue perfecting their understanding of the Bible, of theology, of philosophy, and other sciences germane to their contemplative life. However this intellectual activity is a personal matter for each one, and each individual will suit his own needs in the matter. While some will simply read in order to nourish their meditation and prayer, others will do research work in certain fields of study, or will help keep the rest of the community abreast of new developments in theology, philosophy, monastic studies, history, and so on. The Abbey provides systematic monastic formation for all the candidates preparing to make vows, and a regular seminary course for those who will go on to the priesthood.

Although the monk has plenty to do, his life remains free from an anxious and activistic spirit. He avoids the temptation to make a *career* out of his work. On the contrary, both intellectual and manual work must be understood only as aspects of the monk's vocation to the praise and love of God. Work, carried out in the right spirit of obedience and detachment, is a form of worship. Study oriented to a deeper knowledge of the things of God not only prepares the monk to pray in choir but is itself a form of meditative prayer. The monk who studies is not only working with his mind but speaking to God in his heart and listening to the wisdom taught by God through biblical and patristic writings. Monastic theology is closely related to life and is a constant return to the sources, to the primary encounter with God in His Word and in faith. The monk does not concern himself only with abstract and technical questions, but relates his theology to the *experience* of worship, love and praise. Hence the truest 'theologians' in the monastery are those who are most truly men of prayer.

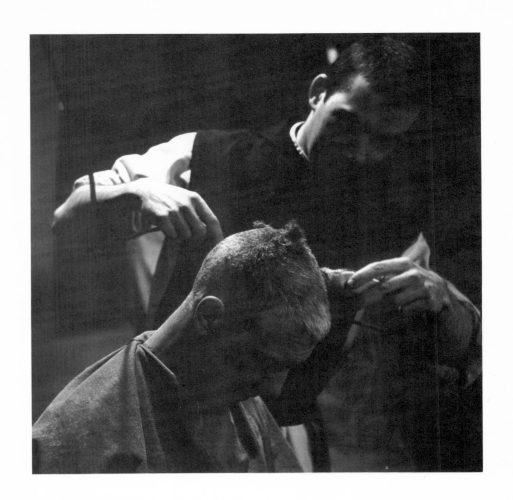

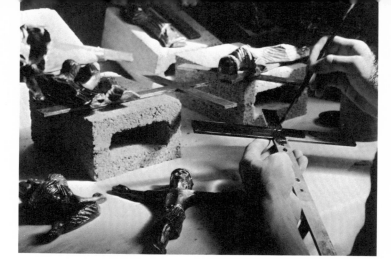

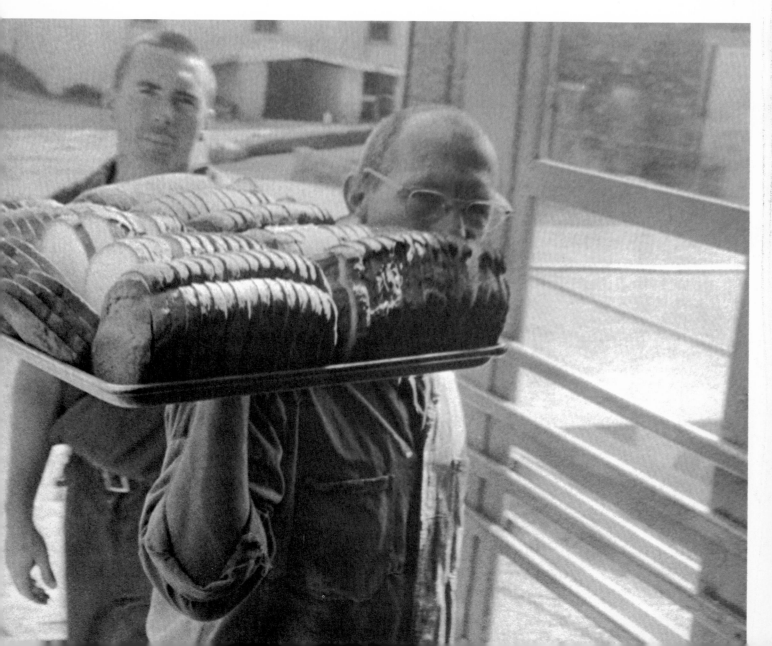

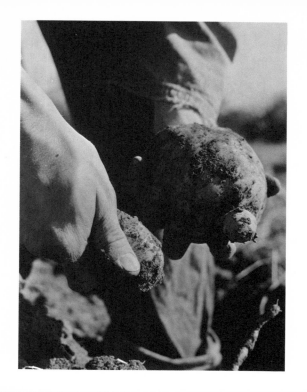

THE LIFE OF PRAISE

The whole monastic life is oriented by its intention to the love and praise of God. Everything the monk does, whether he eats or drinks or sleeps or works, reads or meditates, prays or sings, is guided by one overall intention: to praise God and to please Him, to carry out His will on earth. Hence every act of the monk becomes in some way an act of worship and an act of love. All is referred to the lovingkindess of God who brought us into being out of love, in order that we may spend eternity in loving Him.

A great part of the monk's day — and night — is spent in formal worship, whether in choir and in the liturgical service of the sanctuary, or in secret and personal prayer.

Liturgy is the common worship of the monastic family, celebrating the sacred mysteries together and participating in the Lord's supper, in order to make present each day the redemptive sacrifice of Christ's death and resurrection in which the Father receives perfect praise. The daily concelebrated Mass gathers the entire community around the altar of God in a solemn and yet simple affirmation of faith and love which sums up and consecrates all the rest of the monk's activities.

Here the monk is perfectly united with his brothers in the Holy Spirit and in the love of Christ. Here he offers his own life and his heart to God in and through Christ. Nourished by sacramental participation in this sacrifice, more closely united to all men, in Christ, he goes forth to live as a more charitable and fruitful member of the monastic community and of the Church. Here, in common with his brothers, he thanks God for his gifts and graces to the whole world, offers reparation for the sins of the world and for his own sins, pleads with God for peace and justice on earth and for the salvation of all men. But above all his liturgical service is one of pure adoration in which he joins with the angels and the Church triumphant in singing the praises of the "immortal and invisible King of Ages." The words of St. Paul sum up the whole prayer life of the monk: "Blessed be the God and Father of Our Lord Jesus Christ, the Father of tender mercies and the God of all consolation." (2 Corinthians 1:3) "To God who alone is wise be glory through Jesus Christ for ever and ever Amen." (Romans 16:27)

In the various hours of the choral office, beginning with the Night

Vigils at two thirty in the morning, the monk chants the psalms, listens to sacred readings, prays and meditates on the word of God. Thus his whole day is consecrated by moments set apart for singing the formal praises of God in psalms and hymns. Having adopted a rule of silence in order to speak to men only when necessary, the monk devotes his voice, tongue and heart to this one purpose above all: the praise and glory of God.

Silent and secret meditative prayer is also a most important part of the monk's life. Here the monk prays alone and in the solitude of his heart, meditates on his reading, seeks God's will by deeply reflecting on the events and demands of his daily life, and even seeks a more ineffable personal union with God in wordless, silent prayer and in perfect self abandonment. Here the ways of prayer become mysterious and sometimes baffling to the one who experiences them: but with faith and trust in God he pursues the way trodden before him by many of the saints, in order to be purified and illumined by grace, and united with Christ in one Spirit. (I Cor. 6:17)

Such is the life of the monk. It is at once traditional and modern. Traditional in its essential pattern, which has been the same for centuries, but modern in the new forms by which it seeks to express itself in the lives of essentially modern men, in the most technologically advanced nation on earth.

The attraction of the life of praise may indeed remain incomprehensible to many people in our time, but it is a personal reality. At all times God calls certain men apart from the ordinary life of secular society in order that they may seek Him, praise Him and love Him, to give themselves to Him alone. In so doing, they do a great service to the rest of men. They stand before God in the place of many who cannot believe in Him. They pray to Him for many who have forgotten how to pray. They intercede with Him for those who do not know how to ask His mercy. They thank Him for the good things He has given to all men — gifts which many never recognize.

The monks of Gethsemani worship God and pray to Him not only for themselves but as *your* representatives. They do not plead for themselves only, but for the whole world.

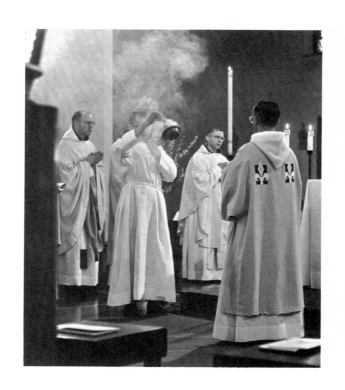

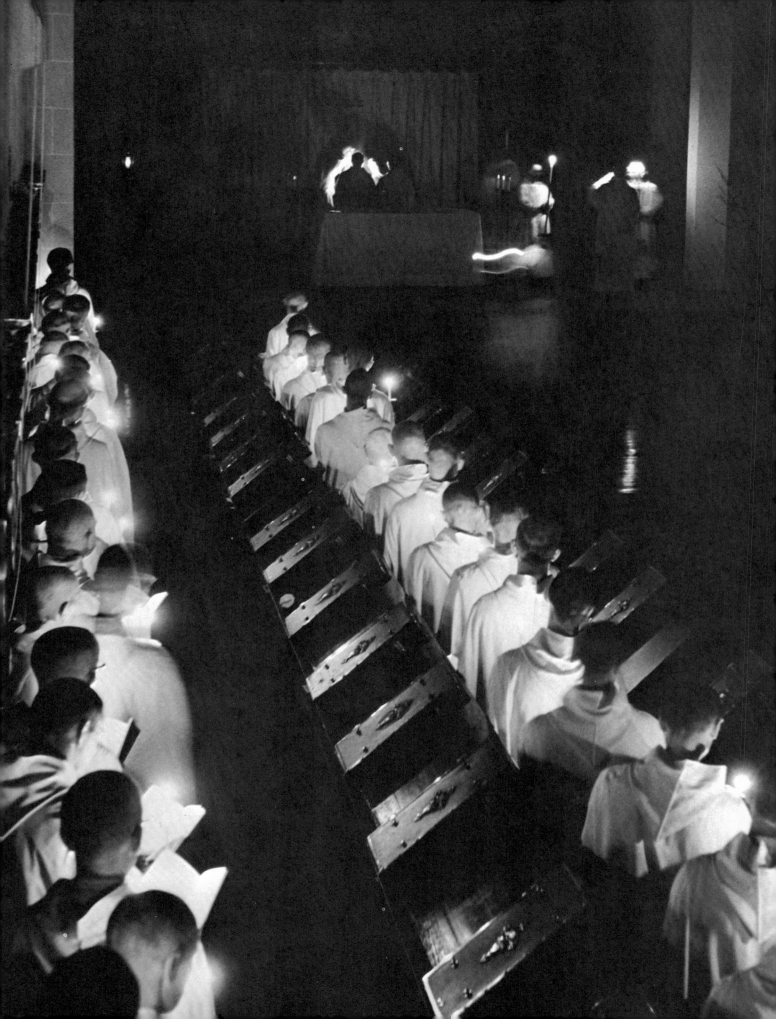

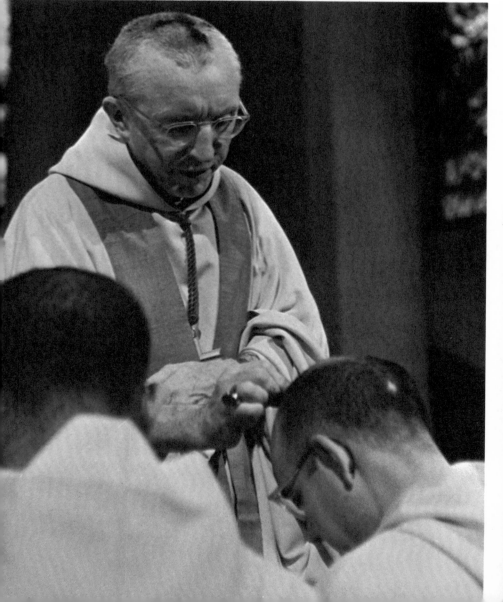